The Holocaust-My Mother's Story

by

Michael Dubiner

Dedicated to my parents who survived, other survivors and to the millions who did not.

Special thanks to John Lopinot, who helped with the conception of the project and in the editing and finally, publishing of My Mother's Story in the Palm Beach Post.

So many of them are dead but surprisingly, some of the buildings they lived, worked and prayed in remain. This is the story of my journey to photograph the structures that were part of my mother's life in prewar Poland.

My parents, Jews, were born in Poland in the first quarter of the twentieth century. Each lost virtually their entire family to the Holocaust. I was born in the United States in 1954, one of two children of these survivors.

As a young child, I knew my parents were different, but I thought those differences were due to their immigrant status and their European accents. As I grew older, I realized that there were much more important differences stemming from their wartime legacy. I felt I too was different. My friends had family. They had grandparents, aunts, uncles and cousins. I had only my parents and my sister.

My mother, Ann Dubiner, was born in 1922 and grew up in the Kazimierz section of Krakow, Poland, the Jewish quarter of the City. Many of the buildings and streets of this section of Krakow remain today largely the way they were when my mother and her family lived there. Some of the structures date back to the early 15th century. What did not survive was the vast majority of the City's Jewish inhabitants.

I was given the opportunity to explore the few remains from my mother's past through a unique program: The March of the Living. This program takes teenagers and adults to Poland from all over the word. Over 5,600 took the trip during the same year that I did. Organizers feel that as many people as possible should see what remains of the Poland of the 1930s, a former haven for Jewish culture and scholarship, which was turned into killing fields and a graveyard for millions of innocents. The time in Poland is followed by a week in Israel, whose rebirth was hastened by the Holocaust. It is hoped that participants will become a new generation of witnesses, helping to insure that this tragedy will never be repeated.

Before this project, I knew little of my parents Holocaust experiences and almost nothing about their family life before the war. I wrongly assumed that Kazimierz, and indeed all other remains of Jewish existence in Poland were destroyed during the war. Jews had resided in Kazimierz for over a century before Columbus voyaged to the Americas. Many of the Religion's most honored and revered spiritual leaders lived and taught there. They built synagogues, cemeteries and other institutions necessary for the proper ritual and spiritual functioning of a pious Jewish community.
In preparation for this trip, I researched the history of the Jews in Kazimierz and my mother shared with me the story of her life before the war and her nightmarish existence as a slave laborer and concentration camp inmate.

However, in September 1939, Krakow was captured so quickly by the Germans that it avoided the prolonged bombing and destruction that devastated other conquered European cities. I have not been able to determine why the Nazis allowed synagogues and other structures clearly identifiable with Judaism to remain standing in Kazimierz. Whatever the reason, the fact that much of Kazimierz remains intact made this photographic exploration possible.

The interior of the Altschul built in 1407. It is now a museum of
the history of the Jews in Krakow.

The Rema, the only synagogue still functioning in Krakow.

The former Izaaka Synagogue was under construction as a museum
at the time I visited it.

The High Synagogue, now unused as a house of worship.

A child plays in the courtyard of the former Kupa Synagogue.

I am not religious, but I was disheartened while spending Friday evening, the start of the Jewish Sabbath on Szeroka Street, the core of the prewar Jewish community of Kazimierz. On this night, fashionable people who had arrived in expensive cars were eating in quaint outdoor restaurants and soaking up the ambiance of the neighborhood. Before the war, these streets would have been filled with Orthodox Jews, hurrying to the scores of synagogues in the vicinity.

Szeroka Street was once the heart of Jewish life. On this Friday night, all that was missing were local, authentic Jews.

On this Friday evening, local children were enjoying a game of soccer in the courtyard of the Altschul, the oldest synagogue in Poland. From the year 1407 until the German takeover in 1939, on any Friday evening, this courtyard would have been crowded with the faithful congregating to welcome the Sabbath with prayer. The playful children were showing no disrespect. There are virtually no Jews left to pray in Kazimierz and the Altschul no longer operates as a synagogue. The prewar Jewish population of Krakow numbered over 60,000, the vast majority of whom perished during the war. That number today is estimated at 200.

Children playing in the courtyard of the Altschul at the start of the Jewish Sabbath.

What remained of Judaism in Kazimierz in the year 2000 are a few elderly Jews, eight synagogues, most of them gutted, a cemetery and a few buildings formerly used by the Jewish community. Each year, tens of thousands of Jews from around the world make the pilgrimage to Kazimierz to get a glimpse of what was once called; "the Second Jerusalem." The truly religious come to pray at the Rema, the only synagogue presently operating as a house of worship. Its weedy cemetery which the Nazis destroyed during the war and which has been restored houses the final resting places of many of the City's greatest Jewish scholars and thinkers. It now attracts the faithful and the curious. Some come to pray, to pay tribute to the dead and to honor the fallen community. Respect for the dead is what drew me there.

The City of Krakow and its restaurateurs have accommodated these tourists by creating a Disney-like facade, the Jewish quarter, without its missing and essential ingredient, the Jews. A police station is discreetly but strategically located in the middle of Szeroka Street to make certain the visitors are not disturbed.

A sign I came across while there demonstrates the tenuous status of Jews in Kazimierz even prior to the war. The sign: erected pre-war, warns the priestly class of Jews called "Cohanim", who traditionally are not permitted by Jewish law to enter cemeteries, that the sidewalk and road have been paved over graves. Obviously, it was not only the Nazis who were willing to desecrate Jewish graves in the City.

Polish policeman walking by a sign warning that the sidewalk and street may be paved over gravestones.

On the doorway of the Tempel Synagogue, only two blocks from my mother's childhood home, someone had painted a Star of David hanging from a gallows, with the words; "Juden Raus" (Jews Get Out) scrawled underneath. It was there that the current contradictory attitudes of Poles toward Jews played itself out. As I photographed the desecration, a young man came to a stop nearby. I pretended to be photographing the facade of the building and not the graffiti, but I was certain that I did not fool him. For the first time in Poland, I was on edge. Obviously, anti-Semitism was alive to some extent in Poland and I did not know this man's intentions. He soon eased my fears when he said in halting English: " I am Polish and it is bad". I was relieved to know that he meant no harm and that he cared about the feelings of a Jew

Scrawled on the Tempel synagogue, Juden Raus", "Jews leave".

A poster of a child was displayed throughout Kazimierz advertising an exhibit and film at one of the former synagogues. It slowly dawned on me that every poster was cut at the child's eye. At the same time, I realized this was no coincidence and that someone had deliberately cut each poster at the same spot.

Advertisements for this exhibit werEvery one of these posters was cut at the eye.

Observant Jews worldwide come to pray at the desecrated and rebuilt cemetery of the Rema.

The broken gravestones that could not be rebuilt make up the "Wailing Wall" of the Rema cemetery.

I was named after my grandfather, Mordecai Dubiner. He was a prosperous businessman who operated a box factory located only a few blocks from his apartment. The factory building was located in an inner courtyard area that I was unable to access despite repeated attempts during my trip. My grandfather and his brother in law owned a building located within walking distance of the Jewish quarter at 5 Dwernickego Street. The building housed apartments, a bakery and a curtain factory. I located and photographed the building that still appears impressive today.

The building that my Mother's family owned, just outside the Jewish quarter in Krakow.

My mother grew up in what was then a luxurious apartment on Miodowa Street, "the Street of Sweet Honey." My exploration of Kazimierz would have been incomplete without being able to see and photograph the inside of my mother's childhood home. As I walked on the street below, I could see children gazing out of the same windows at which my mother once stood. I made several unsuccessful attempts to explain to the mother and grandparents of the children what I wanted, but I was met with suspicion and hostility. One evening, with the help of a translator and the payment of some much needed money, I was allowed entry to photograph the interior of the apartment one evening.

Children peer from the window of my Mother's family's former apartment.

Despite it's somewhat run down condition, I could tell that it was once a residence of some elegance. The design was that of a railroad flat, no hallways, with one room leading directly into the next. Where light penetrated through the windows it was bright, but other areas were somewhat dinghy. I scoured the apartment for any sign, any possible connection to my mother's past. Of course, after over 60 years, there was none.

My head ached as I tried to suppress my tears. After all those years my mother's loss was finally tangible to me. And so I wept. That was just the first day that I cried in Poland. Visiting the buildings of my mother's past, and seeing and photographing the concentration camps and other sites of death, torture and destruction, my every subsequent day was filled with tears for my family and for all the other lost souls.

The view out of my Mother's window.

My mother's family was Orthodox, as were most of the Jews living in Kazimierz. They kept a kosher home and celebrated the Sabbath as a day of rest and prayer. Their home proudly displayed an ornate Sabbath candelabra, a decorative Hanukkah menorah and other decor typical of a religiously observant and successful Jewish home. The present decor of the apartment also reflects the deeply religious beliefs of the current occupants. A painting of Jesus hangs prominently in the back room, located so that it can be seen throughout much of the apartment. I felt it was only fitting that prayers continue to emanate from that home.

My mother had no interest in religion. On Saturdays, when the pious of Kazimierz went to pray, she would go to a friend's house. She quickly changed out of her Sabbath finery and played ball or went to the movies.

A back room in my Mother's apartment displays images of Jesus and a photograph of the Pope.

My mother graduated from high school in the early summer of 1939. After an idyllic vacation in the mountains with her family, she was eager to begin her first job, working as a bookkeeper in her father's factory. She never had that chance. On September 1, 1939, my mother heard the bombing which signaled the German invasion of Krakow. Six days later, the Nazi takeover of Krakow was complete.

Life in Kazimierz changed immediately and dramatically. Germans and their collaborators began accosting, beating and sometimes killing the easily identifiable religious Jews on the streets. My grandfather shaved off his outward sign of piety, his small beard, as an act of self-protection. Soon he was forced to close his factory and his building was taken from him.

On March 3, 1941, the order was issued declaring that Krakow was to be "Judenfrei," Jew free. Some, including my mother's family, were required to move from their homes into the newly created Jewish Ghetto in the Podgorze section of the City. Others were deported from the City, most never to be heard from again.

My great grandmother had a stroke almost immediately after being forced into the Ghetto. My mother describes, with evident emotion, the family helplessly watching her Grandmother die for three days in the tiny apartment assigned to them, unable to secure any medical care. My great grandmother, Baila Dubiner, thus became one of the very first to lose her life to the Nazi ghettoization policy in Krakow. Given what she otherwise would have faced, her death in this manner may have been a blessing in disguise.

The Germans took great care in the construction of the Ghetto walls that imprisoned the remaining Jews of Krakow. The walls were designed to echo the shapes of Jewish tombstones, rounded on the top. Of course they were also covered with barbed wire. They were obviously designed to terrorize as well as to imprison the inhabitants. Only small fragments of these ominous walls remain. When there, I photographed a long forgotten section of the wall. In the background is the hill on which Oscar Schindler viewed the final destruction of the Ghetto.

The Ghetto was made up of approximately 16 square blocks. At it's maximum population, it held more than 20,000 inhabitants. An apartment complex designed for 10 people housed 100. My mother describes the place as crowded but tolerable. Despite the conditions, life went on. My mother met a young man with whom she fell in love and became engaged. Unfortunately, within half a year, her fiancé was deported to a death camp. My mother faced so much tragedy and trauma then and since that she cannot even remember her fiancé's name.

An abandoned swing set built just outside the Ghetto walls still remained for me to photograph.

One day, my mother returned from work to learn that her parents; her older brother and her fiancé had been deported from the Ghetto after a major roundup of residents. Her parents were selected for deportation but her older brother was not. People saw him choose to accompany his parents to what he certainly must have known would be his death. After a frantic search, my mother located her younger brother. At 14, he, like my mother had been at work, his absence had spared his life for a short time.

My mother never knew the date on which this deportation took place or even where her family was sent. During my research for this trip I learned from records that the family was deported on October 28, 1942. The majority of the approximately seven thousand Ghetto residents transported on that date were taken to the Balzac extermination camp and were killed within weeks. The remainder were taken to the Auschwitz-Birkenau concentration camp where virtually all met their deaths. I decided to photograph the Auschwitz- Birkenau complex, which is only 30 miles from Krakow. Portions of these camps have been preserved and I was able to extensively photograph the sites where some of the worst horrors of the Holocaust took place.

On March 13, 1943, my mother and two thousand other Ghetto residents were transferred to the Plaszow concentration camp. She was fortunate as the next day the Ghetto was liquidated and the remaining residents were either killed on the spot or shipped to death camps. Plaszow was located in a suburb of Krakow and was built on the grounds of a large Jewish cemetery. It was where my Mother's grandfather had been buried. Plaszow is the concentration camp that was depicted in the movie, "Schindler's List."

The inmates of Plaszow were terrorized by the ruthless Amon Goeth, who my mother refers to as "king of the concentration camp." My mother was a slave laborer, demolishing gravestones and then carting them in wheelbarrows to be used as paving stones. My mother witnessed hundreds of killings and innumerable beatings in Plaszow. One incident that my mother could never forget, involved a Jewish woman with an injured hand who took pity on my mother. The woman allowed my mother to rest for a short time and took her place at the wheelbarrow. It was this woman's misfortune that Goeth came by as she was pushing a wheelbarrow, which was not fully loaded. My mother watched as Goeth shot the woman in the head for her "crime." My mother's guilt at being the indirect cause of this kind woman's death is still evident as she tells the story today. One day, my mother's younger brother, who was also imprisoned in Plaszow, was transferred and was never heard from again.

Eventually, it was my mother's turn for transfer. She spent two days in a packed cattle car. People eliminated where they stood, as they could not reach the primitive toilet facility that had, in any event overflowed shortly after the trip started. The stench and heat were almost unbearable. Some people licked the accumulated moisture off of the cattle car walls and many died during the trip. One such cattle car forms the core of the Holocaust Museum in St. Petersburg, Florida.

My mother was transferred to Skarzysko Kamienna, a concentration camp that supplied slave labor for an ammunition factory. Many Jews worked with a powder that was poisoning them. Some prisoners referred to them as canaries as the powder turned their skin yellow and eventually killed them. My mother's job was to assemble bullets, all night, every night. Eventually, in order to keep the Jewish slave labor force ahead of the Russian army, the Germans transferred my mother to yet another concentration camp, this one in Chenstlahow. This camp also housed an ammunition factory.

My mother never dreamed that she would leave the camps alive. The constant mental and physical cruelty and fear demoralized most of the inmates, my mother included. In January 1945 Chenstlahow was liberated and my mother was physically free. It is certain she will never free herself from the memories.

She describes her survival as a miracle. There was also something else which allowed her to survive, pure luck. She herself says; "I was just lucky. I did nothing special to survive. It was only luck. The few people who survived were lucky, that's it."

After liberation, most of the remnant of the Jewish population of Kazimierz returned to Krakow in the hopes of locating surviving relatives. My mother's search was fruitless, as the Nazis had killed all her immediate family. Upon her return to Kazimierz, my mother was happily came upon a woman who formerly had worked for her father. The woman asked how many people in my mother's family survived. My mother told the woman that she was the only survivor. The rough translation of the woman's response was; "That is one too many". This incident and continuing Polish anti-Semitism and violence shocked my mother to her core and she departed Krakow a few weeks later, never to return. Most returning Jews left because of similar experiences.

The remaining images, before the concluding text are some of the death camps operated by the Nazi's that I photographed. While I cannot be certain that any of my relatives died in the camps that I photographed, they were killed in one or another of these factories of death and slave labor.

At the entrance to Auschwitz, a Polish tourist photographs her family as a keepsake of her visit.

A mountain of shoes remains.
Unless you look at one, the human toll escapes you.

Prosthetics collected from Jews were destined to be recycled to the German home front.

The entrance gate as seen from the inside of Birkenau.

Birkenau had wood and brick barracks in separate areas.
These are the toilets in the wooden barracks.

This stove provided heat for the prisoners in the bunks lining the walls, three layers high.

Light casts a strange shadow in this brick building that formerly housed inmates.

Showers at Mydonic concentration camp.

Mydonic concentration camp; even then, in full view and smell of Lublin. "What could they possibly be burning there?"

My mother fled to Austria to a Displaced Persons camp. She knew the name of only one American, President Truman. She wrote the President, explaining her plight and asked for his assistance in locating an American uncle she had heard about as a child. Word of her situation somehow reached her uncle who wrote and told my mother that only one of her European relatives, her first cousin, Moshe, had survived the war. She had met Moshe twice before the war, when he had traveled to Krakow on business. One day, my mother saw two men looking around her apartment. One of them was Moshe who had independently contacted his uncle and learned that my mother had survived.

My mother and Moshe, who was later to become my father, quickly fell in love and married I regret I never really learned much about his family, his childhood and his experiences during the war. Of course, I do know that his entire family and his prewar fiancée were killed. He never knew where or how they met their end. When my father died on June 10, 1998, my mother not only lost a husband, she lost her only surviving relative from that time of her life.

My sister, Gina, was born in a displaced person's camp in Austria in 1948. My parents came to America in 1948 when my sister was three months old. Their only possessions were a handful of photographs that their uncle had received before the war. One is of my father's sister. She is beautiful, yet somehow there is sadness in her eyes. In my mind's eye I often see her visualizing what lay ahead. But of course, no one could have imagined what was to come. There are no pictures of my father's parents and I can only imagine how they might have looked. My mother has pictures of her parents and older brother, but none of the younger one. The only other things that remain of those times are the memories, so many of them bitter, and the structures that I have see and that now I have photographed and explored.

My parents at their wedding in the Displaced Persons Camp in Austria.